T0193009

Flip, Float, Fly

Seeds on the Move

by JoAnn Early Macken
illustrated by Pam Paparone

Holiday House / New York

For my mother, who has always encouraged me to grow —J. E. M.
For Richard —P. P.

Holiday House would like to thank Amy Litt, Director of Plant Genomics and Cullman Curator at the New York Botanical Garden, for reviewing this book for scientific accuracy.

Text copyright © 2008 by JoAnn Early Macken
Illustrations copyright © 2008 by Pam Paparone
All Rights Reserved
HOLIDAY HOUSE is registered in the U.S. Patent and Trademark Office.
Printed and Bound in December 2020 at Toppan Leefung, DongGuan City, China.

The illustrations were done in acrylic paint.
www.holidayhouse.com
10 12 14 16 18 20 19 17 15 13 11

Library of Congress Cataloging-in-Publication Data
Macken, JoAnn Early, 1953–
Flip, float, fly : seeds on the move / by JoAnn Early Macken ' illustrated by Pam Paparone. —1st ed. p. cm.
Includes biographical references.
ISBN 978-0-8234-2043-8 (hardcover)
1. Seeds—Dispersal—Juvenile literature.
I. Paparone, Pamela. II. Title.
QK929.M23 2008
581.4'67—dc22
2006037278

ISBN 978-0-8234-3758-0 (paperback)

Take a breath and blow
on a fuzzy dandelion. *Whee!*
One puff sends seeds soaring.
Like small, soft feathers,
they parachute up in the sky.

Maple seeds whirl and twirl in a breeze.
FLIP, FLUTTER, *float*!
The wind lifts them up and off of the tree.
Away they fly like shiny green helicopters,
spinning and spinning.

Tumbleweed plants
grow as round as globes.
In autumn their stems snap off.
On the flat, open prairie, they *ROLL, ROLL, ROLL,*
sprinkling their seeds as they tumble.

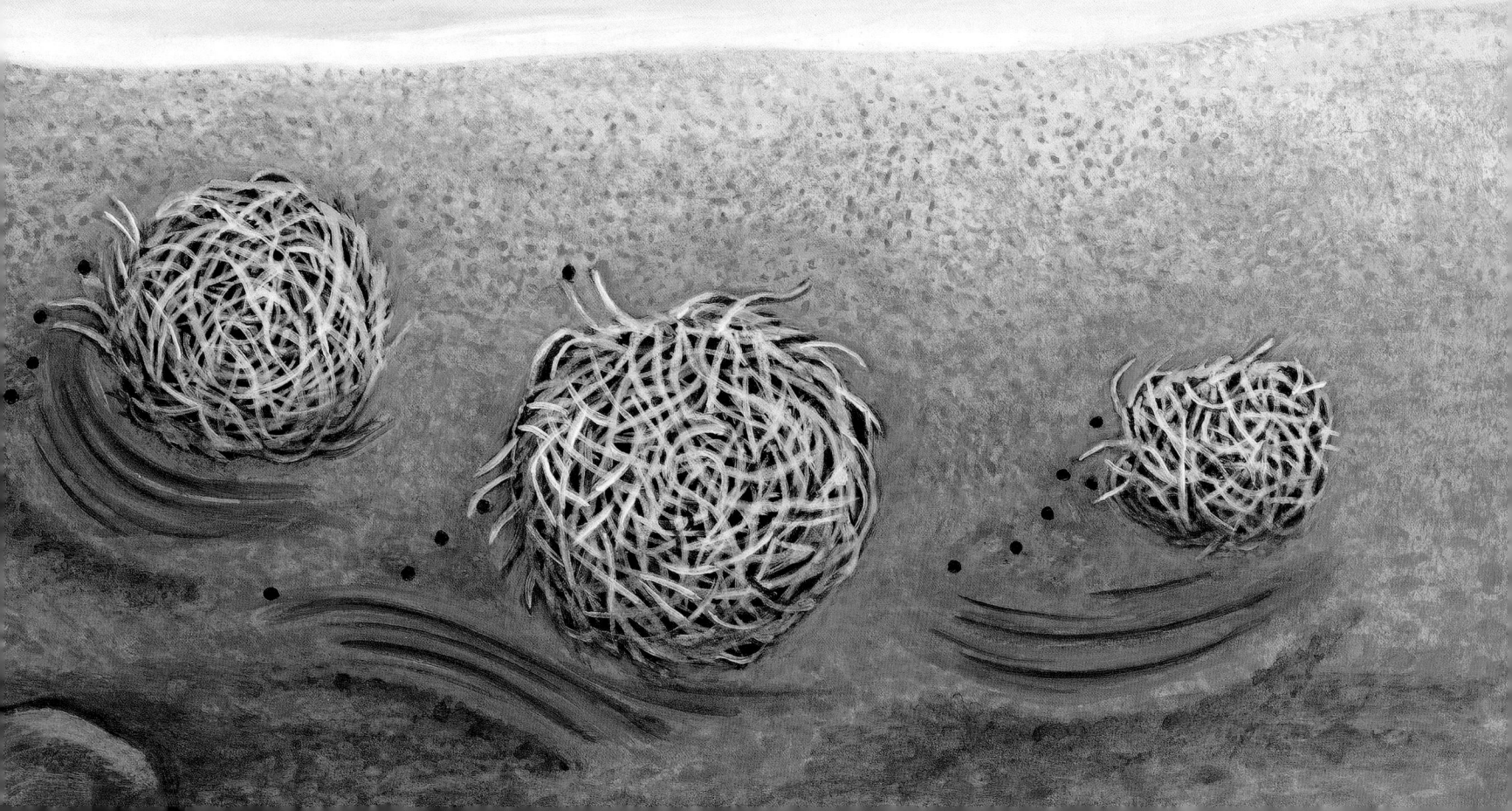

Basswood tree fruit clusters
twist in the wind.
Dangle and DANCE!
In winter they drop.
Like sailboats, they glide
on the smooth, slick snow.

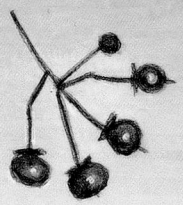

Locust tree pods look like long, brown smiles.
They dry, split open, and curl apart.
Carrying seeds, each side scoots along,
sliding on slippery ice.
SKITTER and *skate*!
Seeds bump off along the way.

Where water flows, it can carry seeds.
Even a raindrop can wash tiny seeds away.
Splash! SWISH! *Splatter!* SCATTER!

The air inside a coconut helps it float.

BOUNCE! *Plop!*

It drops into the ocean

and drifts away on the waves.

Some seeds move on their own.

Poke a touch-me-not seedpod in fall.

POP! *Fling!* The pod explodes.

The seeds are flung.

A wild oat seed
curls up in the sun like a comma.
The seed straightens out when it rains.
WIGGLE! *Jump!*
One way, then the other.
It works its way into the ground.

Animals move seeds around, too.
A bat finds a feast in a fig tree
and wings away with the seeds inside.
The seeds pass through its body unharmed
and fall to the ground in its droppings.

A squirrel scurries
to gather up acorns
and bury them to eat later.
But does it use all the food it collects?
No! Lost acorns can grow
into strong, shady oak trees.

Burdock
flower
seeds

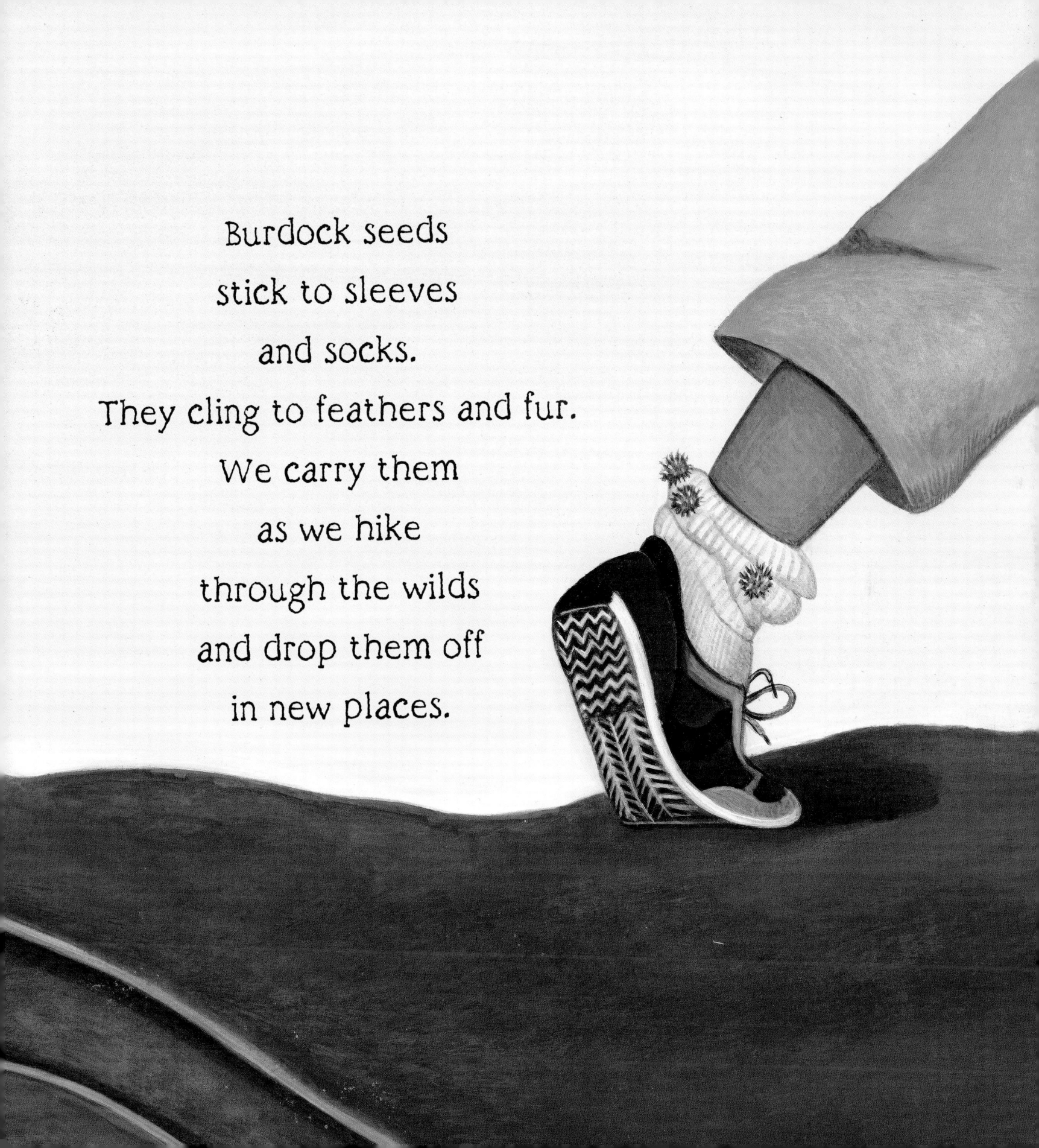

Burdock seeds
stick to sleeves
and socks.
They cling to feathers and fur.
We carry them
as we hike
through the wilds
and drop them off
in new places.

People buy seeds
from garden shops.
Friends and neighbors
trade them and share.
Plants and seeds travel
on ships, trains, and airplanes.
Seeds on the move zoom over oceans,
across cities and countries,
around the world.

People plant seeds
in gardens and flowerpots.
They tend the seedlings and watch them grow.

Sprouts! Shoots! Leaves and roots!
Flowers bloom and new seeds form,
beginning the cycle again.

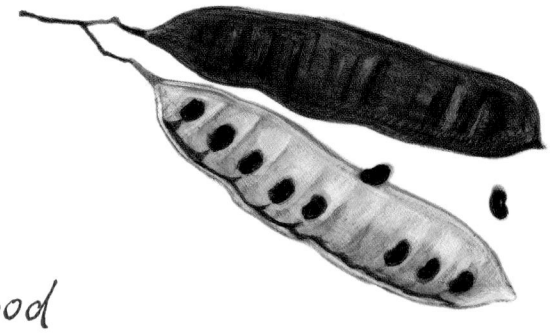

Seedpod
a fruit that holds many seeds, which are dispersed when the seedpod dries and splits open

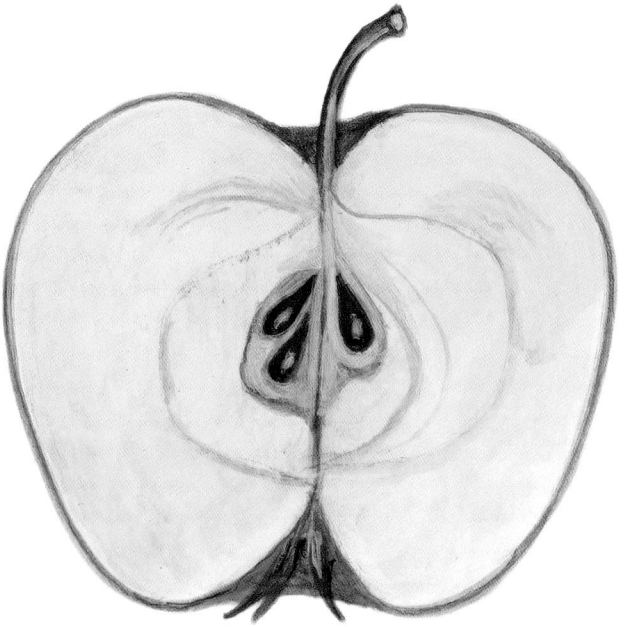

Fruit
a part of a plant that holds the seeds

Seed
the part of a plant that can grow into a new plant

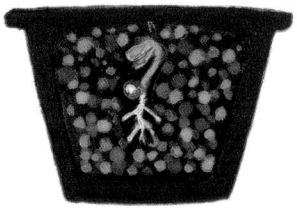

Shoot
new growth on a plant

Sprout
young growth

Seedling
a young plant grown from seed

Nut

a fruit or seed
with a hard shell

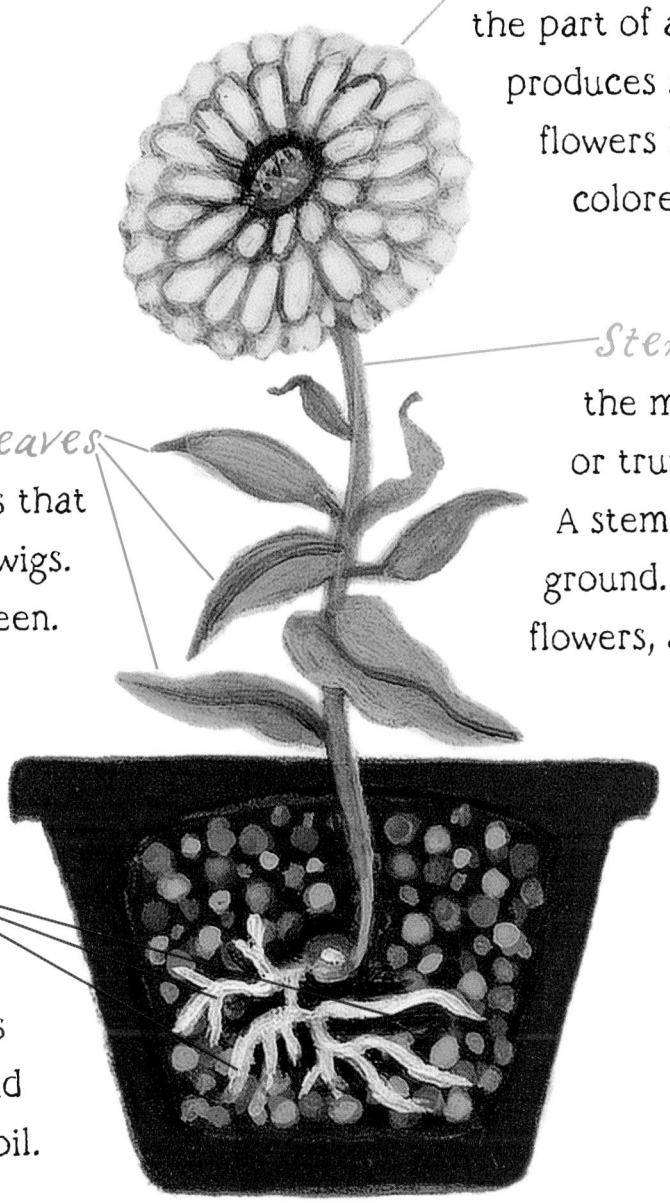

Flower

the part of a plant that produces seeds. Most flowers have brightly colored petals.

Stem

the main stalk or trunk of a plant. A stem grows above the ground. It supports leaves, flowers, and fruit.

Leaves

the flat, thin plant parts that grow from stems or twigs. Most leaves are green.

Roots

the parts of plants that grow underground. Roots hold plants in place and soak up water from the soil.

Apple seed

Tomato seed

Impatiens seed

Corn seed

Notes

Many seeds cannot sprout where they form. Why not? Too many seedlings would crowd the same spot. Layers of leaves would block the light. New plants and old would all send out roots. Tangles of roots would compete for water.

How does a seed get from place to place? An animal, wind, or water might carry it. Or it might move on its own.

Many seeds end up in places where they cannot grow. A seed needs a home with the right light, soil, and amount of water. It may land in a spot with perfect conditions. Then it can sprout into a plant, grow, and make seeds of its own.

Sunflower seed

Pea

Pumpkin seed

Peach pit

Cherry pit